WORSHIPING
Through the
TEARS

WALKING WITH THE FATHER THROUGH
GRIEF, SORROW, AND LOSS

MICHAEL BURDICK

WESTBOW
PRESS®
A DIVISION OF THOMAS NELSON
& ZONDERVAN

WestBow Press books may be ordered through booksellers or by contacting:

WestBow Press
A Division of Thomas Nelson & Zondervan
1663 Liberty Drive
Bloomington, IN 47403
www.westbowpress.com
844-714-3454

ISBN: 978-1-6642-2625-8 (sc)
ISBN: 978-1-6642-2624-1 (e)

Library of Congress Control Number: 2021904525

Print information available on the last page.

WestBow Press rev. date: 03/12/2021

CONTENTS

First and foremost, to the Lord my God and heavenly Father. Through Your grace, love, and compassion, You have allowed me to find my true identity through Your Son, Jesus Christ.

> Let the words of my mouth and
> the meditation of my heart
> Be acceptable in Your sight,
> O Lord, my strength and
> My Redeemer. (Psalm 19:14)

To my loving wife, Mindi, and my sister-in-law, Dawn. This project started with the passing of your mother. Thank you for your encouragement and support to bring this message to others. I offer this work in her loving memory.

And finally, to that sweet twelve-year-old soul. May the angels continue to rejoice over your presence in Heaven.

ACKNOWLEDGMENTS

A special thanks to the many members of Coast Hills Church. Your love and support have been key in helping me realize the true meaning of worship. Words may fail me to express the level of love and gratitude I have for you. I am sincerely blessed to be part of this wondrous family. I offer this work in the loving memory of our friend and sister Connie.

INTRODUCTION

Times of grief, sorrow, and loss can stir up a whole host of emotions. From sadness and disbelief to anger and confusion, managing our emotions in a manner that enhances our walk with God is the focus of this book. Learning to walk with God through these times is difficult. To some, the concept may even be foreign.

As believers, we have little difficulty dropping to our knees in prayer during times of grief and sorrow. However, it becomes too easy, albeit natural, to center our prayers around asking for and receiving deliverance from our sadness. Though asking God for deliverance is not wrong or forbidden, it can certainly set us up for potential disappointment as our sole focus. Studying this topic from a purely scriptural standpoint, I have learned that God wants nothing more than to be our Father. He wants to rejoice with us in times of success and happiness. Conversely, He wants us to fall into His arms and allow Him to comfort and love us through times of despair. If the only purpose God had for our lives was to automatically remove our anguish each time we experience sorrow and loss, we would have no need for the relationship with Him He so greatly desires.

When my children were young, nothing made me more fulfilled than to hold them when they cried. Though I was incapable of removing the pain of the skinned knee or the disappointment they were feeling from a bad outcome in their day, just knowing that they allowed me to hold them and comfort them made me feel like a true father. I believe this is what our heavenly Father must feel every time we seek His comfort more than asking for mere deliverance. As you will see in this book, God rejoices when we rejoice, but He also weeps with us when we weep. He longs to provide the comfort and compassion needed at our most desperate times. And when we accept that level of love from the one who loved us first, our faith is rewarded far beyond anything mere deliverance can provide.

Trusting in God to be our compassionate Father fosters a deeper relationship with Him. In a sense, it is the purest form of communion we can offer a God that wants nothing more than to commune with us in all aspects of our day and lives. This is why He sent His only begotten Son. Jesus died and was resurrected not just to bring us salvation from our sins but to bridge the gap between us and a God that greatly yearns to be our Father. As our God, we worship Him for what He has created and His ultimate plan to save us for Himself for all of eternity. But as our Father, He achieves a personal relationship based on unconditional love and respect that He wholly desires us to experience. In return, we find a deeper level of worship that cannot be found sitting in a church just because it's Sunday. But more importantly, that deeper worship fosters a love for our Father in us that can carry us through the most trying of times in our lives, as well as finding real joy during the best of times. Above all, we achieve our primary goal of deliverance so that we can ultimately see the Son shine at the end of the storm by merely worshiping through the tears.

Worshiping Through the Tears was initially drafted in outline form as a small-group study for my church members. Born out of being a support to my wife, sister-in-law, and family through my mother-in-law's passing, the church readily accepted this as a much-needed small-group ministry. What I found was this could be used not only in a group setting, small or large, but also as a self-study for anyone desiring to learn more of what scripture offers on the subject. Whether you are going through a time of grief, sorrow, or loss, *Worshiping Through the Tears* can support a believer to do the following:

- explore examples of grief and sorrow exhibited in scripture
- appreciate what it means to weep with those who weep
- actively pray without ceasing in times of grief
- learn to actively glorify God through worship, even in the most challenging times and darkest hours

As we learn to and actively press into God as our Father in times of despair, not only will we find comfort and strength for our walk and situation, but ultimately, it will create in us the ability to be a support to those around us in their times of grief. So, I thank you for taking this journey with me into a deeper connection with God as our Father. My only hope is that God will be glorified through your faith in Him so that He can be glorified through you—not only to allow God's blessings on your life but also for the benefit of those around you through your testimony of expressed faith.

A BIT ABOUT ME

I am just an average guy. Nothing special. No major credentials to sport behind my name. I haven't been to seminary. I have never been the founder of a charity or mission-based organization. I have not single-handedly saved anyone, nor am I close to offering a cure for any disease that ravages this world. As the British may say, I am just an average bloke trying to get through this thing called life, like everyone else around me—or so I thought.

I was the fourth and last child in a family of six. My parents were married my entire life until the passing of my father in 2004. My childhood was not marred by any physical abuse in the home. For the most part, folks would probably say my siblings and I turned out well. My parents did what they could to instill proper values and morals in me. We were not wealthy by any means. As my mom always said, "We may not have had everything we wanted, but we always had everything we needed."

My journey with the Lord started when I was in grade school, going to a local church on the Oregon coast. I found the experience to be refreshing, as I was accepted for who I was and seen for my life's potential. It was not long before I was baptized. Looking back now, I know that I believed in Jesus at the time of my baptism, and

I wanted to commit my life to Him. What I did not know were the necessary next steps to move from commitment to a relationship with God. At the time, I did not realize how this would significantly shape my adult life.

Soon after that, I began going to my mom's church. I spent time in junior high as her personal assistant as she would conduct Sunday-morning children's church. Like most, I learned all the Sunday school Bible stories and about this man named Jesus. And let us not forget all those simple songs we would sing every week, always acknowledging how much this Jesus loved me. As I progressed through my high school years, I became highly active in the youth group. Those were some of the best times of my life. I was provided many opportunities to serve in so many ways that service to others became a way of life—a vital lesson I thank God for teaching me that early in my life. The church was nondenominational and firmly rooted in God's Word. Faith in God was not in short supply with this group of amazing people. However, like most churches in the eighties, their primary focus was salvation. Spread the Word, secure the conversion, and move on to the next lost soul needing to hear the Gospel. Now please understand, I assure you that the members were dedicated Christians, with their faith in the Lord adequately placed. What I lacked was never truly grasping the relationship piece. In other words, I did not understand the true meaning of worship. As a result, it was too easy to walk away from the church and God once I began my early adult years. And so I did.

I spent the next thirty years wandering through life, doing the best I could. My son was born out of wedlock when I was twenty-three. My son's mother definitely deserved better than I treated her back then, as the stress of fathering a child without the means or life skills to handle the job greatly affected how I responded. Thankfully, that amazing woman accepted my offer of marriage, and we embarked on a journey that just passed its thirtieth anniversary at the time of this writing. I do apologize to all those at our wedding who lost the bet we wouldn't make it. But I am blessed to have proven you all wrong (you know who you are). Not long after our wedding, my wife and I welcomed our daughter into this world. And there you have it. A family of four, with champagne tastes on a beer budget, moving through life just like everyone else.

Raising our children was interesting, to say the least. However, I spent most of their early years working to provide for the family. I do not regret that in any way, but I know my wife has memories of our kids that I do not possess because of the long hours required to maintain my job-focused, provide-for-your-family mentality. And as time went on, through the ups and downs of my life and marriage, God slowly became more distant until He was relegated to pleasant memories of times had in my youth.

I can honestly say that my forties were the worst time for me mentally. I allowed myself to believe that my life was halfway over, that I didn't have much to show for it, and the remainder would be a slow downhill journey to the grave. As a result, this time in my life was as internally miserable as one could guess. I was definitely not the best husband, I was a more distant father, and I failed to allow much to bring me joy. I spent a lot of the time seeing my failures, thus minimizing my successes. Then I started thinking about God—but not the way one would hope. I saw Him more and more as this distant being who may have created the world, but at no time did I see Him as my Father or, for that matter, a deity who was even interested in me. It got to the point that I actually started to rationalize Him not existing at all. God was just an illogical being created by people needing to hold on to a hope they could not prove for the sake of justifying our existence on this third rock from the sun we call earth. What was even odder is that I would make my arguments to Him as if I were attempting to convince God Himself of His nonexistence.

At this time, my marriage was tough. My wife had become incredibly successful in her career as a nurse; my kids were grown, going to college, and starting their own lives. Dad, the provider, in a sense, was no longer necessary. My leg of the race was over. The baton had been handed off, and life was relegated to an amount of time that simply needed to pass. Our financial difficulties and most of our marital strife were self-imposed at the hands of yours truly. And all this time, I was using it as evidence that God did not exist. My wife had started the conversation of returning to church, yearning for more than where our lives were and had become. Yet I was resolved to consider the request only, trying to figure out how I was going to fake that one.

And then one day ... while reading the morning news, I came across a story about a twelve-year-old girl. She apparently got off the school bus and started to walk home when a man grabbed her, pulled her into some bushes, and stabbed her to death. I became outraged. I was mad beyond my own comprehension. And boy, did God hear from me. I spent the next week or so (literally) screaming at the top of my spiritual voice. I blamed God for not intervening. I blamed God for not protecting this innocent child He created, a person I did not even know. But I did not stop there. Several days into this spiritual rant, I eventually got to the point that I accused God of not being worthy of my praise (not my finest hour). I literally told Him, "How dare You call yourself worthy when You idly stand by and allow this atrocity to occur."

I do not profess myself to be one who hears the audible word of God. But I know He speaks to me in thought, through song, and definitely through the words and actions of others. As soon as I had made my case that God was not worthy of my time and praise, He finally had His say with me. Suddenly one morning, after finishing my daily rant, I experienced the most audible thought I have ever had, never doubting this was from God Himself. God simply said, in a loving and graceful way, "Now that we have my nonexistence cleared up, listen to your mother and your wife, get your butt back into church, and I promise you, we will work on the rest." And so began my journey back to not just knowing about God but experiencing that personal relationship I could never grasp as a younger man.

Testimony is a fantastic thing. But I have always had a slight discomfort listening to others share their testimonies when they end their story at the turning point. Please don't get me wrong. Telling of our conversion is critical to testify of God's grace, mercy, and love. But I have come to appreciate that every believer's testimony is constantly being written. There is no end to how God is working in our lives, and therefore, we should never stop sharing, as Paul Harvey would say, the rest of the story.

My journey since has been primarily focused on grasping my true identity. I have learned that I am not just God's creation but a unique, one-of-a-kind individual created in His image. Like you, I am royalty. I am a child of the King of kings. And because of the amazing and loving sacrifice of His Son, Jesus Christ, I have salvation. And with salvation, I have been ushered into a purpose beyond my abilities. I have been given the gift of the Holy Spirit, who through me can produce the relationship with God—the Father I need and so desperately want to know more and more. I am His kid. He has shown me mercy and grace I could not earn, and He freely gives it out of love—a love that is not based on circumstance or status but deserved as a believer who accepts His Son as our only means of access to His true greatness.

Recently, our senior pastor brought profound revelation to my walk. He said that the single most desire in his heart is to have God come through him, not from him. And God does come through him. This has become my life's true ambition. And in that pursuit, I was led by the Holy Spirit to understand and appreciate the need for worship, the desire to commune with the Lord daily—to not only talk to Him but to be still and expect a response.

Looking back over my life, I know exactly when I walked away from God. But I can also see that even then, God never walked away from me. And now my future is entirely in His hands. For more of my testimony, well, I guess you will have to check back at a later date because it remains unfinished. Am I perfect? No. Am I average in God's eye? Far from it. Will I let Him use me to fulfill His purpose? Absolutely.

Yes, God does exist. He loves me just as much as He loves you.

We are His workmanship, purposed for His work for His glory. And all I can say is thank You, Jesus, for Your willingness to sacrifice Yourself so my average can become God's extraordinary.

I have had my sorrows. I have had my disappointments just as much as I have been the disappointment to others. But my story, my testimony, is not over. God has never quit on me, nor will He quit on you. He is worthy of our praise. He is worthy of our worship. And I will continue to worship even when I must spend time worshiping through the tears.

BEFORE WE BEGIN

Finding answers to stress has been the driving force behind the existence of counseling. Counseling, in our modern world, comes in many forms. We have counselors for just about every stress one might face, from financial counselors to marriage counselors, to all other subjects, such as addiction, anxiety, and depression. Now, before you get the wrong impression, let me be clear from the beginning. I believe that God provides people with the passions of their heart and provides them with what the scripture refers to as giftings. Those drawn to practice as counselors, in my mind, are no different. They serve a much-needed realm, helping those seeking answers and strategies to overcome their stressors. The occupation of counseling should never be viewed as not from God.

According to the US Bureau of Labor and Statistics, the number of jobs in 2019 under the category of Substance Abuse, Behavioral Disorder, and Mental Health Counselors was 319,400. More strikingly, the ten-year Job Outlook, or growth rate, is rated at "25% (Much faster than average)."[1] IBIS*World*, an industry research firm founded in 1971, reports that the occupation of behavioral therapists will be an $8.8 billion industry by 2020.[2] In addition to the professional world, the church has always offered counseling services in various forms. Safe to say, the need has never been greater.

People have been seeking the advice of counselors as far back as the Old Testament. To hear directly from God, leaders and priests had to elicit the counsel of the prophets. When the Israelites were led out of Egypt, their marching orders from God were delivered through His servant Moses. From Isaiah to Malachi, these books detail the direct words of God through these prophets. When Jesus paid the ultimate price through His death and resurrection, He ushered in the ultimate counselor for each believer through the gift of the Holy Spirit. What is interesting here is when Jesus was proclaiming the coming of the Holy Spirit, He referred to Him as "the Comforter" (John 14:26). Paul, in Romans 8:26, tells us, "Likewise, the Spirit also helps us in our weaknesses," testifying to the Spirit's role as not just a counselor but as an intercessor for times when we don't understand how to pray effectively.

Seeking the counsel and advice of others is also scriptural. The most poignant of commandments on this subject can be found in James 5:13–16. Here we are directed to pray for those who suffer, sing songs with those who are cheerful, and even confess our sins to one another so that mutual prayer can bring about healing. Paul, in 1 Thessalonians 5:14, tells us to "comfort the fainthearted, uphold the weak." The overall point is that God, through the work and guidance provided by the Holy Spirit, may very well lead us to the paths of others we can trust to help us through times of grief, sorrow, and loss.

So, with all these avenues of help and support, why worship? Wouldn't it make more sense to merely seek out others, read the self-help books, and follow advice from those more credentialed than I am? Simply put, counseling should be viewed as an option—and a valuable one at that. But worship, as a believer, is not only our right; it is our responsibility. It is the foundation of our faith put into action. In short, worship is not an option; it is the starting point— the starting point for all phases in our daily life, both good and bad. As we will see in greater discussion later, the command in 1

Thessalonians 5:16–18 to "rejoice always, pray without ceasing, in everything give thanks" is because "this is the will of God in Christ Jesus for you." Our worship is God's will for our lives—in good and bad times, in sickness and health, and in all phases of our daily lives. Counseling may be an option, but worship is a must.

Worshiping Through the Tears is focused solely on the need for worship. As many respected ministers and pastors have preached throughout time, worship is a directional, heart-driven mindset that should invade every situation we encounter. Worship brings us daily in the presence of our God, who desperately wants to be our Father. The one we can trust and look to when nothing or no one else seems to be of any help. The one to look to with praise for the many blessings received. And the one to turn to when all hope seems lost. Worship is not a replacement for the counsel and advice of others. Worship is the place where we belong from beginning to end.

As stated in the introduction, *Worshiping Through the Tears* started as and is designed to be a small-group study. Should you choose to use this material in that setting, a few words on the structure. First, each session is designed to be conducted in a ninety-minute time frame.

- Open Review of Previous Week
  10 Minutes
- Worship and Prayer
  10 Minutes
- Message
  15 Minutes
- Open Share/Discussion
  15 Minutes
- Worship and Closing Prayer
  10 Minutes
- Fellowship/Sharing/Prayer
  30 Minutes

As you can see, each weekly session should open and close in some form of worship. Whether it be open share and praise for blessings or joining in music, time for worship must happen. If you elect to use this as a self-study, enter and close each chapter in a time of personal worship.

Fellowship time at the end is also critical. Though this time frame will fluctuate from session to session, connecting with our brothers and sisters in Christ is essential to building a sense of community and trust among one another.

Finally, I offer a word of caution. *Worshiping Through the Tears* is a scriptural view on how to bring God into your situation. By doing so, you allow Him through His grace and love to provide strength, peace, and ultimately a sense of joy that He is walking with you through this time in your life. Humankind's nature, and one of the enemy's tactics, is to try to get our minds stuck on the situation. If we allow ourselves to be stuck in pain, we spend time reliving the grief and sorrow over and over. As a result, we fail to let God's healing positively affect our lives.

The driving force behind getting stuck is the misconception that we are designed to *get over* our grief, sorrow, and loss. God's healing is designed to help us work through our grief, sorrow, and loss so that our testimony of His love can be a demonstration of His daily presence in our lives. "Getting over it" is not required. Getting through it allows us not to get stuck and continuously live in pain. Though we will always have the memories, worship enables the Holy Spirit to use them for our benefit, regardless of when in life they resurface. This is one of the main focal points of *Worshiping Through the Tears*.

So, before we begin, what is worship? A simple question whose answer seems to be universally understood. But let us take a moment and ensure we are all working off the same understanding. That way, we can eliminate any unnecessary assumptions.

The word *worship* is found multiple times in the Bible. The word *worship* indicates a physical and mental posture toward God. In a sense, worship is paying homage to God with a full sense of reverence and awe. True worship requires heartfelt, heart-driven attention to the Lord—a moment in time where the believer presents him or herself before God for the sake of communing with Him as a Father. Though many attribute worship as a time spent in a church service, worship actually occurs anytime and anywhere we choose to be present with our Father. If we can accept this generalized definition of worship, we can also accept that we are engaged in worship every moment our hearts and minds are focused on God.

How we worship is not as significant as actually spending time in worship—be it a moment of prayer, song, meditation on his Word, or praising his name and thanking Him for the beautiful sunset. In any of those circumstances, I submit you are in a moment of worship. And that is the key to *Worshiping Through the Tears*. Worship is a function of our hearts, directing our love and devotion to the only God that will never leave or forsake us. Giving praise to the one true God for the many blessings we enjoy. And displaying trust through faith when we fall to our knees, wanting only to be held and comforted by our loving Father. Many agree that worship is easy when in seasons of joy and peace. But leaning into God during the seasons of grief, sorrow, and loss and presenting ourselves at His feet when the need is more significant than we can bear is what I simply refer to as *Worshipping Through the Tears*.

TELLING GOD
HOW YOU FEEL

Many have the idea that prayer is a structured address to God—words carefully crafted to achieve some lofty goal or make sure that others will accept our utterances as religiously correct. However, when you look no closer than the book of Psalms, King David obviously did not hold this viewpoint. In fact, David was very personable in his prayers, petitions, and praise to God. The difference is apparent. Those in the former pray out of religion, where David prayed from the heart from a place of relationship. This is why his psalms are so treasured throughout the world of believers.

In looking at grief, sorrow, and loss, David represents a strong example of standing in a position of worship while facing the toughest of trials and tribulations. To validate this point, let us look closely at Psalm 13. In this psalm, something is going on in David's life that has produced a tremendous amount of sorrow. Though we do not know for sure the cause for his suffering, just reading through the first four verses shows the depth of that sorrow.

How long, O LORD? Will You
   forget me forever?
How long will You hide
   Your face from me?
²How long shall I take
   counsel in my soul,
Having sorrow in my heart daily?
How long will my enemy
   be exalted over me?
³Consider and hear me,
   O LORD my God;
Enlighten my eyes,
Lest I sleep the sleep of death;
⁴Lest my enemy say,
"I have prevailed against him";
Lest those who trouble me
   rejoice when I am moved.
⁵But I have trusted in
   Your mercy;
My heart shall rejoice in
   Your salvation.
⁶I will sing to the LORD,
Because He has dealt
   bountifully with me.

There are so many takeaways from these six verses. First, it is evident that David has no issues crying out to God. On the surface, it would appear in the first two verses that God is being accused of hiding His face from David and his circumstances. But in reality, it is obvious that David is so sure in his relationship with his heavenly Father he knows he can boldly say what is on his mind and be honest with God about how he is feeling. Looking closely, David is not accusing God of being the cause of his sorrow. Instead, I can picture that David is spiritually being held close by God, who is allowing David to display his sorrow honestly.

Just two verses in, and we can clearly see that with relationship comes security to be open and vulnerable with our Father. God knows He is not the cause. God knows He has not hidden His face from David. But instead of cutting David off in midsentence or rebuking him for blasphemy, God is being a father. He is present, and He is listening. This controlled, loving approach continues into verses 3 and 4 as David turns his dialogue into a plea for intervention.

This turn in David's discussion with his Father should be quite familiar to most of us. How many times do we quickly turn our prayers into telling God what we think we need? Moments of great sorrow and grief usually bring about pleas to God not only for deliverance but for the exact type of rescue we're sure we need. We fool ourselves in thinking that we have the answer, and if God would only agree with our position on the matter, all would be resolved sooner rather than later.

But then something unique happens in the final two verses. David abandons his pleas and reaffirms his devotion and trust in the Lord. In short, he reverts to worship. David is no longer concerned with how God will deliver him from his sorrow; instead, he lays his whole life back into God's hands. Even in his sadness and grief, David ends the psalm declaring he will sing. David is in immense internal pain, and his answer is to sing to the Lord.

Jesus Himself exhibited this type of reverent expression for his human-based feelings just before His arrest. In Mathew 26:36–42, Jesus is pouring out His heart to His Father, displaying an immense amount of grief over the events to come.

> [36]Then Jesus came with them to a place called Gethsemane, and said to the disciples, "Sit here while I go and pray over there." [37]And He took with Him Peter and the two sons of Zebedee, and He began to be sorrowful and deeply distressed. [38]Then

He said to them, "My soul is exceedingly sorrowful, even to death. Stay here and watch with Me." ³⁹He went a little farther and fell on His face, and prayed, saying, "O My Father, if it is possible, let this cup pass from Me; nevertheless, not as I will, but as You will." ⁴⁰Then He came to the disciples and found them sleeping, and said to Peter, "What? Could you not watch with Me one hour? ⁴¹Watch and pray, lest you enter into temptation. The spirit indeed is willing, but the flesh is weak." ⁴²Again a second time, He went away and prayed, saying, "O my Father, if this cup cannot pass away from Me unless I drink it, Your will be done."

This time in Jesus's life is challenging to comprehend fully. On the one hand, we see Jesus sorrowful and speaking from a place of great distress. On the other hand, Jesus is the Son of God, living in the full knowledge of how the story is going to end. Yes, Jesus knows He is going to die, and His death is going to be in the most horrible and painful manner imaginable. But He knows the outcome. If anyone had the ability to rise up and demonstrate faith without fear, now would be the time. He could have simply stood tall and laughed in the face of His crucifiers. But He doesn't. He feels sorrowful, and He wants His friends close at hand. And above all, He wants His Father in Heaven to offer the same thing David wanted in Psalm 13, deliverance. But just as David did, Jesus places all His trust in God, uttering the words, *not as I will, but as You will*. Such reverence for His Father. So much trust. A pure example of faith in action. For David, this makes sense. But why does Jesus act in the same manner, given His status as the Son of God?

First, theologically, Jesus is furthering His ministry of only doing what the Father tells Him, only saying what the Father says. But why the sorrow and grief? Is it possible that Jesus, allowing His human side to show, is modeling for us the same trust and adoration for

15

His heavenly Father as we should do in times of great despair? Is Jesus using this as a teaching moment for both His disciples and us? I believe this can be seen as the truth. Jesus even goes back to His disciples and wakes them up, urging them to pray, trying to impress upon them the severity of the situation and the need for earnest prayer. But even then, He returns to his Father in prayer. Jesus is showing the real significance of prayer and worship in times of great sorrow and grief. And He is doing so in the same manner David displayed in Psalm 13. In short, both had no difficulties telling God how they were feeling. But they both allowed those feelings to send them into a time of worship, trust, and affirmation of their reliance on God's comfort and strength.

When you are suffering loss, experiencing genuine sorrow and immense grief in your life, how do you choose to treat God? Do you look to Him as just a rescuer, or can you sit in His lap, allow Him to hold you, and feel the strength in your relationship? Can you open up and just let God listen to how you feel? Telling God how you feel is not a sin. As a matter of fact, it is what He truly desires. Consider this thought. Though we all agree that we should not yell *at* God, is it OK to yell in His direction? Is it OK to cry in His lap? Is that level of trust and adoration for His comfort and strength merely a form of worship? I am comfortable answering yes to all the above.

Worshiping God daily brings strength to the relationship. And in doing so, it increases trust in Him as our Father, not just our holy creator. And in that moment of true, honest communion with Him, all His promises can come forward, and the blessings only He can provide work in and through us to give us the strength to face the challenge.

CHAPTER FOCUS:

1. Worship, worship, worship.
2. Give yourself permission to feel how you feel, and be willing to take your feelings to God in prayer.
3. Supporters should always pray for their loved ones and ask only how they can help them worship God.

UNDERSTANDING
SORROW AND GRIEF

When it comes to defining sorrow and grief, there are multiple usages and corresponding definitions in scripture. With each use, we learn the deeper reality of these feelings. Examples abound in both the Old and New Testaments.

In Genesis 42, Jacob's sons need to journey back to Egypt due to the famine of the time. On this return trip, they were required to take their brother Benjamin with them. Under the belief that Joseph was already dead, Jacob prohibited his sons from taking the youngest, Benjamin. In anticipating the worst possible outcome of losing Benjamin, Jacob describes his feelings in verse 38:

> ³⁸But he said, "My son shall not go down with you, for his brother is dead, and he is left alone. If any calamity should befall him along the way in which you go, then you would bring down my gray hair with sorrow to the grave."

The word *sorrow* in this passage is the Hebrew word yậgộn

(yaw-gon).[3] This is best defined as the grief of the heart. This is the same word David used in Psalm 13:2, discussed in the previous chapter.

Jacob's use of sorrow is interesting because, unlike David, who was actively experiencing sorrow, Jacob is anticipating the level of distress he would experience under a set of circumstances that have not yet occurred. Anticipatory sorrow, though self-inflicted, is quite common. A stressor happens, our minds begin to dwell, and before you know it, we walk ourselves into a space of sorrow that we label as the worst-case scenario. Often, that worst-case scenario never materializes. We generally write it off as worrying too much, or laugh it off, thinking ourselves to be silly for thinking like that in the first place. But look at the issue a bit deeper. What is really happening when we anticipate sorrow and react accordingly is we are taking our eyes off our heavenly Father. And as our stress strengthens, our trust in Him weakens.

Though we cannot shut off our feelings, recognizing this cycle early on is the best means of working through the anticipation of what might happen. If the worst possible outcome can lead us back into worship, thus exercising our faith by trusting God, then that heartfelt sorrow becomes more manageable. Worshiping at this moment lets God know that even though our heart is troubled, our confidence in His perfect plan will override any scenario that follows, even the worst case. Though future circumstances are always unknown, worshiping through this sorrow helps us maintain the commandment in 1 Thessalonians 5:16–18:

> [16]Rejoice always, [17]pray without ceasing, [18]in everything give thanks; for this is the will of God in Christ Jesus for you.

Changing the outcome now becomes less critical. Being in the presence of the one who will never leave or forsake us becomes our only focus. In doing so, our walk and communion with the Father increase, allowing His love, strength, and peace to flow through us in the manner only He is capable of blessing.

In John chapter 16, Jesus is trying to prepare His disciples for His pending death and resurrection. Though the disciples were confused as to what Jesus was trying to forecast, He attempts to comfort them by saying this in verse 22:

> [22]Therefore you now have sorrow; but I will see you again and your heart will rejoice, and your joy no one will take from you.

The Greek word *lupē* (loo'-pay)[3] denotes a great sadness, a heaviness of sorrow. On the one hand, He is preparing them for this tremendous level of sorrow over His physical loss. But on the other hand, Jesus is explaining the power of His resurrection. He comforts them with the prophecy that they will rejoice at a level no one can take away upon seeing Him again. What a promise. What a focus. Pending loss, causing such a heaviness of sorrow, ending in heartfelt rejoice untouchable by humans.

Think back on times in your life when you experienced a significant loss—loss of a loved one; loss of employment; loss of connection with close friends. Allow yourself long enough to focus on the level of grief and sorrow you experienced. At that moment in time, were you looking for joy? Were you expecting to end the day with your heart rejoicing? If you are anything like me, probably not. But what if this promise is more than just a one-time circumstantial act only to be realized by His disciples when they saw Jesus resurrected? What if this is a perpetual promise extended to all believers? And can daily worship, both in good times and bad, turn this promise into a reality? Let us follow some simple scriptural math and see if we can answer these questions.

First, scripture repeatedly reminds us that God is love. God wants nothing more than for us to love Him with all our heart, mind, and soul, otherwise known as daily committed worship. Through the sacrifice of His only begotten Son, we are ushered into a personal relationship guided by the Holy Spirit. The fruits of the Spirit include peace and joy. With that said, is it hard to see that worship leads us to experience God's steadfast love for us? And in that experience, the Holy Spirit's gift of peace can invade our daily circumstances, both good and troubled. And in that peace, our hearts can find joy—not just a simple pleasure but a pure form of joy that no one can steal. Is it becoming easier to understand the power and significance of worship?

Grief and sorrow are normal human emotions. But what is more important is these emotions are from God, given that we were created in His image. As we have seen, even Jesus experienced these emotions while on earth. But Jesus did more. He not only felt the way we may feel at times, but He also modeled for us the best way to manage our sorrow and grief. Jesus allowed His sorrow to help Him find the peace and the courage to walk to the cross for you and me. He did so by talking with His Father, worshiping His Father, and trusting in His mission to do only what the Father told Him to do and say only what the Father said. As a result, we are welcomed into the same throne room to experience all that God has for us, so we can also have the courage to walk through any storm our lives experience.

Let us end this session revisiting 1 Thessalonians 5:16–18.

> [16]Rejoice always, [17]pray without ceasing, [18]in everything give thanks; for this is the will of God in Christ Jesus for you.

In times of great sorrow and grief, this can be the hardest of the verses in the Bible to realize. First and foremost, we cannot stop praying. Communion with the Lord daily is the vital ingredient. We do not thank God for our circumstances; we thank Him for allowing us to choose to have Him in all our situations. And with God in all our experiences, situations, and times of sorrow, we can always rejoice in knowing the Holy Spirit is there to provide us that much-needed comfort. It is here we can realize the true meaning of hope—that confident expectation that God will be glorified through us no matter what, and as a result, we will be blessed immensely.

CHAPTER FOCUS:
. . . .

1. Worship, worship, worship.
2. Embrace 1 Thessalonians 5:16–18.
3. Supporters, ask God to show you how you can be an extension of the Holy Spirit's role of comforter.

PRAYING IN TIMES OF SORROW AND GRIEF

Few believers can argue that prayer is one of the essential parts of our daily relationship with God. In the previous chapter, 1 Thessalonians teaches us that prayer is "the will of God for us through Christ Jesus." In other words, this is God's desire. To be in a state of constant communication with His children is what He wants. And He wants nothing more than for us to share in the same desire. As I have gone deeper into my study of prayer, I have been amazed at what the Holy Spirit has highlighted to me in showing the significance and need for constant prayer.

Now, I realize that we discussed the need and importance of talking to God openly versus just lobbing Him with pleas for deliverance in an earlier section. God wants to hear our praise. He wants to know that we see Him as our one true God, and He wants to know that our hearts yearn for His love and grace. But prayer is not a one-sided conversation. To allow for open, honest dialogue, He also wants to hear our petitions. In short, God wants to listen to both sides.

To illustrate this potential dilemma, let us first start by looking at the characteristics of prayer Paul teaches us in Romans 12:12.

Paul uses the Greek word *proskartereō* (pros-kar-ter-eh'-o),[3] defined as *being earnest toward* or *continuously diligent*. The NKJV translates as continuing steadfastly.

> [12]rejoicing in hope, patient in tribulation, continuing steadfastly in prayer.

Here, Paul is indicating the need to pray in earnest. A need to be focused and honest in our discussions with God. But he also implies a sense of diligence when we pray. To say that we pray to God is one thing. But to pray earnestly in a continual, diligent manner is the hallmark of effective prayer. Jesus demonstrates this same level of earnest prayer in Luke 22:41–42. Here, just prior to His arrest, Jesus has taken His disciples to be with Him as He prays.

> [41]And He was withdrawn from them about a stone's throw, and He knelt down and prayed, [42]saying, "Father, if it is your will, take this cup away from Me; nevertheless not My will but Yours, be done."

Here Jesus is openly showing his anguish in asking for His Father to remove this cup. But in the end, He places His full faith in His Father by submitting to God's will over His own. He appears to be demonstrating that to be genuinely open and honest with God, telling Him how we feel, includes trusting Him with our desires in the matter.

Paul furthers this point in Philippians. He makes it perfectly clear that telling God what we need and want is also essential. This is the intent of the Greek word *Deesis* (deh'-ay-sis),[3] supplication or petition, that Paul uses in Philippians 4:6–7.

> [6]Be anxious for nothing, but in everything by prayer and supplication, with thanksgiving, let your requests be made known to God; [7]and the peace

that of God, which surpasses all understanding, will guard your hearts and minds through Christ Jesus.

First, he substantiates that prayer should be a continual effort when he says, "in everything." Using both words, "prayer and supplication," he emphasizes that requests to God need to occur but only through a thankful heart.

Now that we have seen both sides of the conversation, let us talk briefly about the power of prayer. Prayer is so powerful. Jesus modeled this issue multiple times in the Gospels. In Luke 22:31–32, Jesus prays for Simon Peter.

> [31]And the Lord said, "Simon, Simon! Indeed, Satan has asked for you, that he may sift you as wheat. [32]But I have prayed for you, that your faith should not fail; and when you have returned to Me, strengthen your brethren."

Now, let us take a moment and add context to this powerful declaration Jesus is making to Peter. Here, Jesus is about to reveal to Peter his pending denial. Peter is ready to do whatever it takes for the sake of Jesus, even "both to prison and to death" (v. 33). But this is the amazing part. Not only is Jesus telling Peter what he is about to do, in the previous verses (31–32), Jesus is trying to tell Peter what has already been done. You see, when faced with Peter falling into the sin of denying Christ, Jesus combats this with prayer. He is not saying He will pray for Peter. Jesus is saying that He has already prayed for his "faith should not fail." Is it not interesting that of all the weapons Jesus has at His disposal to defeat the advancement of the enemy, here His weapon of choice is prayer?

The words "and when you have returned to Me" are Jesus prophesying victory. The denial has not happened yet; Jesus knows of what Satan will attempt; Jesus prays specifically for Peter, and now Jesus is declaring victory over a battle that has yet to begin. Why? The end of the verse. Jesus wants Peter to know that he will go through the denial and, as a result, will suffer great internal sorrow for that act. But Jesus also knows that because of His prayer, Peter will return to Him. So, He gives Peter instruction that when he gets back, "strengthen your brethren." Jesus is simply saying, "Do not let this time change your identity, focus, or purpose." Peter was His rock, and as such, Jesus knew how important it would be for Peter to resume his role as a source of strength to others. He desperately wanted to show Peter that he would survive this attack with his identity intact. With his identity secured, Peter would have the ability to maintain focus on his gift of being a strength to others.

The sin, the sorrow, and the attempt Satan made have no power against the prayer of Jesus. Dare we ask, since Jesus cared so much to pray for Peter at this time, what prayers is He offering to God on our behalf? What situation are you facing or about to meet that Christ has already prayed for and declared victory over? How much love does Jesus have for you to pray in such a manner?

If you see these questions as challenging to ponder, consider that the Holy Spirit also prays for us. Paul tells us this in Romans 8:26:

> [26]Likewise the Spirit also helps in our weaknesses. For we do not know what we should pray for as we ought, but the Spirit Himself makes intercession for us with groanings which cannot be uttered.

To me, the emphasis is on how constant the state of prayer is and needs to be. Here the Holy Spirit is focused on praying for us in our time of weakness. The Spirit acts as an intercessor to keep the conversation moving forward when we don't know what or how to pray. He does so to strengthen us, provide comfort, and what I choose to believe is effect the necessary changes our spirit needs. What a tremendous ally we have in the Holy Spirit. To rely on and use this ally for God's glory in our lives is an enormous blessing God provides, especially in a time when we are cloaked in sorrow and grief.

So, now that we have seen characteristics of prayer and the power of prayer, this discussion would not be complete if we did not work through the challenge of the timing to His answers. As I have maintained, prayer is more than just constantly seeking deliverance from our sorrow, grief, or time of loss. But there are times God chooses to show up in a mighty way and provide us with much-needed deliverance in ways we simply cannot explain. Believers call this immediate reversal of fortune a miracle—a sign or wonder of the true power and grace of God. And believe me, we serve a powerful God who is more than capable of making the blind see, the lame walk, and yes, even the dead rise. But then comes the question of why He chooses not to deliver on time, 100 percent of the time? Why does God choose to change circumstance on a dime, thus providing immediate relief and deliverance on one occasion, but on another, we seem to have to walk through the fire? I believe there are times in our lives when the process is more important than the outcome. Let me illustrate.

In my working career in case management for members of the Oregon Health Plan, I spent six weeks going through formal training on the subject of motivational interviewing (MI). In this training, one is instructed in the art of conversation that starts with open, honest dialogue for the sole purpose of gaining understanding. Without understanding an individual's needs, beliefs, and barriers to change, we cannot truly guide them in achieving the goals set for themselves. But to overcome their personal barriers, we must slowly over time influence them into what the MI calls "change talk." Change talk is not designed to be a bait-and-switch type of persuasion. Change talk is intended to applaud and support the individual's desire and reasons for making a change. By helping them verbalize a better understanding of how they feel, they can better focus on reasons to change instead of the overwhelming task of making a change. Using change talk makes it easier to guide an individual in navigating the personal barriers preventing positive change.

Is it possible that in times when the answers to prayer seem to be nonexistent, God is asking for our trust in Him through faith to continue the conversation? Is it possible that God, through the work of the Holy Spirit, is trying to evoke in us a sense of change talk? And how can He help us navigate this change talk on a conversation we have not had?

I believe this is what Paul is discussing when he tells us to "let your requests be made known to God." As we have discussed, open and honest communication is what God desires in all of us. He not only wants us to trust in Him, but I believe God wants it to be known that He trusts us to be openly transparent with Him. Once again, our focus becomes less about the outcome and more about the process. Having the power of the Holy Spirit work change talk into our lives starts with open dialogue, yes. But look at the verses again.

> [6]Be anxious for nothing, but in everything by prayer and supplication, with thanksgiving, let your requests be made known to God; [7]and the peace that of God, which surpasses all understanding, will guard your hearts and minds through Christ Jesus.

The purpose of the process is not a selfish intent on God's part to get us to think differently. In these verses, the goal is to let God protect our hearts and minds, thus reducing anxiety through our exceedingly difficult times. When you can see God's work in this light, how can you not bring your prayers and supplications to Him with a thankful heart? And when we embrace the process more than the outcome, does the meaning of Romans 5:3–5 become more apparent?

> [3]And not only *that*, but we also glory in tribulations, knowing that tribulation produces perseverance; [4]and perseverance, character; and character, hope. [5]Now hope does not disappoint, because the love of God has been poured out in our hearts by the Holy Spirit who was given to us.

I offer one final thought on this vital subject of prayer. This is mainly directed to those who want to support ones suffering a time of sorrow, grief, or loss. In my study, I have come to see prayer in two different settings. The first is praying FOR people. The second is praying WITH others. Let me illustrate.

We all offer and agree to pray for our church family members, friends, and loved ones. I cannot stress the significance and importance of taking on this role. It should never be viewed as a consolation to not being able to aid in another, more tangible way. Offering to pray for someone is huge. My only suggestion is when you offer to pray FOR someone, take it seriously. Pray in earnest. Pray continually steadfast. Take them to the altar of the Lord in the same manner of compassion and concern you would take a child to the doctor. Never underestimate the power of prayer, but also do not fail to own up to your offer to pray for someone else.

Praying WITH others is a uniquely different setting. Prayer still needs to be earnest. But there would seem to be an additional level of power released when we pray WITH others. Consider Jesus's words in Mathew 18:19–20.

> [19]"Again I say to you that if two of you agree on earth concerning anything that they ask, it will be done for them by My Father in heaven. [20]For where two or three are gathered together in My name, I am there in the midst of them."

I see two main takeaways in this passage. First, when we pray together, it is essential that our prayers agree. Now, I am confident that theologians and church pastors can take that issue alone and create volumes on precisely what that means and how to get there as a group. For the sake of our discussion, I shall not dive into that one. Regardless, group prayer needs to be from a place of agreement.

The second but most important and powerful takeaway in this passage is Jesus's location during group prayer. Jesus promises to be "in the midst of them." In short, when we pray together, Jesus is in our prayer group, praying right along with us. How much more powerful do you need your prayer life to be than to have the Son of God standing right next to you, with His head bowed, hands folded, eyes closed, joining in on the conversation with the Father? Such a breathtaking promise by a loving Savior.

To sum this up, see both settings as powerful and much-needed places of prayer. I liken it to the following. Praying FOR you is what I choose to do when we are not together, and I will never underestimate the power that setting provides to my prayers. But praying WITH you is what we do when we are together praying in Jesus's name. That setting, as you can see, places Jesus right between you and me, focused solely on mutual communion with the Father. Thank You, Jesus, for bestowing upon us the ability to stand WITH You in prayer.

CHAPTER FOCUS:

1. Worship, worship, worship.
2. Prayer is one of the most necessary components to worship.
3. Prayer is so powerful that Jesus and the Holy Spirit continue to pray for us.
4. Praise God for the immediate answers. But also trust Him through the process.
5. Supporters:
   a. Honor your promise when you offer to pray FOR others. Never underestimate the significance your prayers can have on the situation.
   b. Never pass up the opportunity to pray WITH someone in Jesus's name. He promises to be in your midst, praying right alongside you.

BEING SUPPORTIVE: WHAT TO DO WHEN THERE IS NOTHING TO DO

A friend reveals that they are going through a tremendous struggle. Maybe it is the loss of a loved one, loss of employment or their home, or even grief over a life circumstance shrouded in the unknown, such as a potentially devastating diagnosis. Whatever the struggle, they have confided in you. You have been sought out to share in their burden. Sound familiar? I am sure all of us at one time or another have been confronted with someone else's grief, sorrow, or loss. Our hearts sink. We are filled with empathy. We want nothing more at this moment than to be a source of strength and comfort. So, we ask, "What can I do to help?" And then the answer comes we hear so often. There is nothing that can be done.

Scripture tells us repeatedly to be supportive by lifting each other up. Trying to be supportive when there seems to be nothing to do can be one of the most challenging barriers to overcome. But when we look at what the Bible tells us, doing something meaningful is not always a physical or visible task. Being supportive actually starts with the proper mindset. Romans 12:15–16 best illustrates this point.

¹⁵Rejoice with those who rejoice and weep with those who weep. ¹⁶Be of the same mind toward one another. Do not set your mind on high things, but associate with the humble. Do not be wise in your own opinion.

I see this as a complex set of instructions. Verse 15 seems to be the easiest. I have met few believers who have any issue with rejoicing in a time of joy or weeping with someone in their time of sorrow. As you can see, verse 15 tells us what we need to do. But verse 16 tells us how we must go about accomplishing this mission. Verse 16 shows us that being supportive starts with the right mindset. "Be of the same mind toward one another" clearly suggests that we first must approach our friend with empathy and compassion. We must be willing to feel what they are feeling and think like they are thinking. In short, this moment in time is not about me.

I realize that the previous statement may be awkwardly offensive. But to be supportive of the one who came to you, sometimes the last thing they need is your solution. The last thing they need is your opinion, past relevant history, or even an idea on how to proceed. I believe there may come a time when some or all of that may be appropriate, but verse 16 clearly states that should not be where we begin. Helping someone, a.k.a. being supportive, is always about meeting their need, not our own internal need to be necessary.

This point is further substantiated in 1 Corinthians 12:24–26.

²⁴ ... But God composed the body, having given greater honor to that part which lacks it, ²⁵that there should be no schism in the body, but that the members should have the same care for one another. ²⁶And if one suffers, all the members suffer with it; or if one member is honored, all the members rejoice with it.

There are so many takeaways in this entire chapter regarding the body and the significance of how each member strengthens one another. For the sake of our discussion, the focus is threefold. First, we must approach our fellow brothers and sisters in Christ with great honor. Not a difficult thing to say and realize. When a friend brings you their burden, they are displaying great honor to you just by the simple act of seeking you out. To properly receive this honor, it must first be viewed as a display of honor. With that proper mindset, honor received becomes honor easily returned.

Secondly, verse 25 states our next step cannot contain or produce "schism in the body." The amplified version uses the word *discord*. In other words, our first response to our friend cannot intentionally or unintentionally cause friction. Now, some of you may quickly dismiss this as impossible to occur. Who would ever purposefully cause any type of discord to a friend cloaked in sorrow and grief? Short answer, no one in their right mind would. But appreciate that an uncalculated response can produce unintended meaning or interpretation. How do we avoid this? Our final point of focus is found in the rest of verse 25. "Have the same care for one another." Honest empathy, inserting yourself in their shoes and feeling how they must feel, is all you need. Allowing yourself to "suffer with" helps you be slow to offer solutions, opinions, or relevant past histories when a simple embrace suffices.

Asking what a friend needs or wants from you is extremely valuable at this very moment. Even if they do not know what they need, just asking is a return of honor. Showing that you are willing to be there and walk with them is delivering proper care. Similar to the discussion on prayer in the previous chapter, this is another time when process trumps outcome. And above all, it helps us accomplish the goal of being like-minded in facing this heart-wrenching time.

As time moves forward, do not underestimate the power of prayer. Time spent in prayer is a form of worship. Taking the time to pray for and with someone can never be seen as a consolation for not having anything else to do. Engaging in continual, steadfast prayer as a part of your time of daily worship opens up a dialogue with God. That dialogue, in turn, allows God to show how the Holy Spirit can and will use you to provide the level of support that is genuinely needed. Please do not offer to pray for someone if you have no intention of following through with the offer. Prayer is too important and necessary to be viewed as a routine casual response to one's situation.

With that said, let us look at what we can tangibly do to be a support, even when we don't know what to do. This very topic brought back a difficult time in my life when I was called to support a close friend and I had no clue what I was doing or going to be able to offer. It was summer, one year after my high school graduation. One of my closest friends had just experienced the loss of his older sister. What was even more painful was she was just as much a part of our church youth group as he and I were. She was a fantastic soul, one year older than her brother and I, and filled with all the promise and potential life had to offer. I remember seeing her just days prior to her passing. I remember hearing the excitement in her voice about her future plans. And just a few short days later, my mother called me at work to tell me that she was gone. Over the next couple of days, the details surrounding her death became known, making the loss even more traumatic. My friend, and for that matter, the whole youth group was devastated.

I have found few things in life more difficult than to support someone going through tremendous sorrow and grief at the same time I am trying to process a similar level of anguish. Couple that with being only eighteen years old, and you can imagine my level of loss and confusion as to what to do next. Within that first week, my friend called and asked if I would come over to his house. He lived close, and it was a pretty short bike ride from my house, so of course, I immediately agreed. I remember telling my mom before I left that I had no clue what I would say or do when I got there. I was so lost. I wanted to be able to say or do something that would have meaning and purpose at this time, but again, I was barely wrapping my head around what had just happened. I knew I was so unequipped to be the support I felt he would need. And my mother, being the remarkable, faith-filled woman she is, simply told me that all I needed to do was be present and let my friend tell me what he needed. I had no clue how prophetic those words would be just a short time after she uttered that profound advice.

I reached my friend's home, and before I could even get partway up the walkway to his door, he emerged with a basketball in hand. He did not say much, but I knew that we were going to spend time in his driveway, proving why he was far the superior athlete than I would ever hope to become. And there we were. Two friends, not talking much, just shooting hoops.

Finally, he spoke. He told me that he was thankful I came over. He revealed how difficult it was to be sitting around the house, watching his mother, father, and younger sister openly grieve. The atmosphere was simply too much for him to bear. And then he said it. He thanked me again for coming over because all he needed at that moment was to "just shoot hoops."

I share this experience to illustrate one point. Sometimes all we need to do is be present. Yes, there will be times our friends will need more. Sometimes they will ask and need your opinion. Sometimes they will want to hear how you went through a similar time in your life for the comfort mutual experience offers. There is a time and place for that, and when the time comes, one should be willing to offer what is asked. But sometimes, all that is needed is your presence. Sometimes all that is required is that like-minded care for one another scripture revealed earlier. Sometimes, the only necessary thing is to just shoot hoops. Diversion can be a powerful tool. Proper diversion is not avoidance. Instead, proper diversion can be a means to refocus and refuel, a chance to clear the mind and find a moment of joy in a time when joyful moments are scarce.

Good diversion can come in many forms. A movie night out. An assault on a spouse's credit card during a day of shopping at the mall. A time of focusing on anything unrelated to the sorrow and grief. The opportunity and willingness to be available in a manner that promotes diversion can mean more than any amount of profound wisdom we can ever think to bestow. Yes, it may be awkward. Yes, it may seem unnatural and out of character. But remember, this is about what they need, not what we think they might need. In short, to be the best support to anyone going through tremendous grief and sorrow means to let the need come to you and act accordingly.

CHAPTER FOCUS:

1. Worship, worship, worship.
2. Ask what needs to be done, resisting the urge to tell them what they need.
3. Offer to help them worship.
4. Pray FOR and be willing to pray WITH.
5. Ask the Holy Spirit to show how He wants to use you most in a supportive role.
6. Being present is providing support, even when it does not look like it.

MEMORIES:
WHO'S DOING THE
TALKING?

Our memories hold different forms and speak to different times and circumstances in our personal lives. For example, I am sure that we have all had a loved one close to us pass away at some point. Be it a friend, coworker, colleague, or family member, we all have someone or some people in our lives who today exist only in our memories. We also hold memories of times or events in our lives that form the basis of our self-perceived identity—memories of times we were successful; times we selflessly helped our neighbors; or even moments when we were the recipients of help and support from others. Conversely, we also hold memories of times and events in our lives we would just as soon erase from our recall—circumstances we regret that can cause us to relive the pain and remorse when those memories quickly resurface.

Memories are enormously powerful, both for our good and for our detriment. Often, when we pause to reflect on one memory, suddenly one, two, or more memories of the same individual or circumstance in our lives surface as well, one building off the other.

Our reactions to these memories will vary. Sometimes we will smile; sometimes a tear will fall; sometimes we allow ourselves to relive the shame and remorse.

Regardless of the type of memory, the real challenge is effectively managing those memories as they emerge to the surface of our consciousness. Suffice to say, happy memories are easy to manage. We easily store these memories into the column of our lives we label blessings. But the tough memories, those memories that seem to haunt us—those guys can indeed wound our spirits and decrease our focus on the Father. Memories like that of the last argument or words said we wish we had not uttered. Or even memories of times we allowed ourselves to be wrapped up in life instead of spending quality time with our loved ones. Those are the more difficult memories to manage. When we fail to manage them properly, we risk getting stuck in the pain and sorrow all over again. The guilt and remorse seem to rule the moment, dropping our focus on what our heavenly Father has to say on the subject.

The first point to realize is that the Holy Spirit is the driving force behind properly managing our memories. I believe scripture clearly shows that memories are an important tool the Holy Spirit uses to enrich our lives through promoting proper focus. John 14:26 says this:

> [26]But the Helper, the Holy Spirit, whom the Father will send in My name, He will teach you all things, and bring to your remembrance all things that I said to you.

Here, Jesus is merely telling us to understand and rely on the role the Holy Spirit plays in our memories. Memories are designed to bring us back to all things Jesus said, thus promoting a need to allow ourselves to remember. Remembrance promotes focus. And focusing on Jesus enables a deeper level of worship.

David drives home this point of focused worship in Psalm 145.

This psalm is a compelling display of worship, revealing the joy and peace that result from praising God. For this discussion, I want to center our focus on verses 5–9.

> [5]I will meditate on the glorious
> splendor of Your majesty,
> And on Your wondrous works.
> [6]Men shall speak of the might
> of Your awesome acts,
> And I will declare Your greatness.
> [7]They shall utter the memory
> of Your great goodness,
> And shall sing of Your
> righteousness.
> [8]The Lord is gracious and
> full of compassion,
> Slow to anger and great
> in mercy.
> [9]The Lord is good to all,
> And His tender mercies are
> over all His works.

Here, David shows that meditation on God's glorious splendor is worship focused solely on the Father. As we maintain our focus, we begin to utter the memories we possess of God's greatness in our own past experiences. In doing so, the Holy Spirit builds off those memories to remind us that His tender mercies are over all His works. One memory, building off another, bringing peace to our soul in a moment of focused worship.

Paul further substantiates proper meditation or focused worship in Philippians 4:8.

> [8]Finally, brethren, whatever things are true, whatever
> things are noble, whatever things are just, whatever

things are pure, whatever things are lovely, whatever things are of good report, if there is any virtue and if there is anything praiseworthy—meditate on these things.

Focusing our meditation is vital to grasp if we hope to ensure memories are received and used to further our relationship with Him. Focused meditation on the works of God strengthens our connection and reliance on Him. The use of our memories for any other purpose is not God's intent or desire for us. The role the Holy Spirit plays in the management of our memories, ensuring proper focus in worshiping our Father, simply cannot be understated.

Looking at Galatians 5:22–23, we get a stronger sense of how the Holy Spirit works in and through us.

> [22]But the fruit of the Spirit is love, joy, peace, longsuffering, kindness, goodness, faithfulness, [23]gentleness, self-control. Against such there is no law.

The role of the Holy Spirit in our lives produces results—results scripture calls fruits. Fruits of the Spirit provide us a great measuring stick we can easily apply in all areas of our daily worship. This is especially true when managing our memories becomes painfully difficult.

In properly processing and managing our memories, we must always stop and consult the source. Through our faith in Jesus, we can easily see that there are only two sources to all things. Either things in our lives are from God, our Father, or they are not from Him. When I think of the question, "What is from God?" I choose to look no further than the verse in Philippians chapter 4 we just reviewed. Let's look again.

> [8]Finally, brethren, whatever things are true, whatever things are noble, whatever things are just, whatever

things are pure, whatever things are lovely, whatever things are of good report, if there is any virtue and if there is anything praiseworthy—meditate on these things.

Here we see that God provides us everything that is true, noble, just, pure, lovely, and of good report. When we correctly meditate on these things, I believe we should see the results or fruits of the Spirit. This notion may be simplistic to those theologically inclined, but not everything in scripture is meant to be complicated. If anything in our lives exhibits any one or more of the attributes listed in Philippians 4:8, and those attributes result in any one or more of the fruits of the Spirit listed in Galatians 5:22, can we agree that thing in our lives is from God?

In further determining what in our lives is from God, consider Jesus's words in John 10:10.

> [10]The thief does not come except to steal, and to kill, and to destroy. I have come that they may have life, and that they may have it more abundantly.

Here, Jesus is comparing His mission to that of Satan's. Satan is the thief, and his only mission is to steal, kill, and destroy. When Jesus is the source we draw from, we experience the life God wants for us in abundance.

So, how does this pertain to memories? Again, a vital step we must take in processing and managing our memories is identifying the source. This is a huge step that easily becomes overlooked in times of grief, sorrow, and loss. As stated in the beginning, memories are powerful. They can make us smile and, even more so, fill our hearts and minds with regret. We all have moments of regret in our lives. We all have said things we wish we had not said and things we did that we desperately want to take back. In a time of loss, it is common to begin remembering the last words spoken, or the last argument had, or even words or thoughts of love that went unsaid. Immediately, we are filled with regret and remorse. We convince ourselves that the one we lost did not know how much they were loved, respected, or admired. And immediately, we are awash in guilt. Sound familiar?

Now let us hold there for just a moment and take that vital next step. Instead of lingering in our guilt and shame, let us seek out the source. Because when you take a memory that produces regret, remorse, and guilt and then compare it to the scriptures listed above, the source is definitely not from God. Regret, remorse, and guilt have nothing to do with the abundant life Jesus promised. And none of those are on the list of fruits of the Spirit. And when you apply Philippians 4:8, one could easily see why these have no place in our time of meditation. Simply put, they are not from God, so none of His purposes are served when regret, remorse, and guilt rule our thoughts.

Now let us apply the opposite. Take the memory that sprang to your mind because of a song, a word from someone, or even a passage. Take that time when one pleasant memory was used to recall the next or even more memories. Even though they may produce a small moment of sadness, how peaceful do you feel when you remember the laugh of a relative long since passed? How much goodness do you experience when you recall the love they displayed to you while alive? And how much joy does God place in your heart when remembering the silly times that made you laugh together when they were alive? These memories easily fit into God being the source.

I cannot stress enough how identifying the source is so critical. If the memories are from God, the Holy Spirit has a purpose to further the abundant life Jesus came for you to have. If the memories are not from God, their only goal is to kill, steal, or destroy.

Take the sorrow of loss out of the scenario for just a moment and let us refocus this matter on our own identity. Recall, if you will, the prayer Jesus spoke of in combating Peter's pending denial.

[31]And the Lord said, "Simon, Simon! Indeed, Satan has asked for you, that he may sift you as wheat. [32]But I have prayed for you, that your faith should not fail; and when you have returned to Me, strengthen your brethren."

Again, Jesus knew that Peter would go through remorse, shame, and guilt because of his act of betrayal. Jesus also knew and declared victory over the battle before it even started. I believe that Jesus also knew Peter would recall this time in his life on multiple occasions. So, He gives him instruction to show that his identity and purpose will remain intact. How many times do we have faith that God can and will use us in His mighty way, only to have the memories of our past creep in to cast doubt? How many times do we think of ourselves as being unworthy because of the things we have done or said? How many times do we allow past regret to get us stuck in that place of pain? These are some of the many reasons I believe God is a forward-thinking Father. A mission-driven God fueled by our acceptance of His opinion of us, not our own. In this light, I have come to appreciate the English Standard Version of Lamentations 3:22–23 even more.

[22]The steadfast love of the Lord never ceases;
    his mercies never come to an end;
[23]they are new every morning;
    great is your faithfulness.

How can we expect ourselves to live in the new if our memories are used to keep us stuck in the past? God wants us in the new so He can help us move forward into our future with Him. No, I am not suggesting we block out our past and fight our memories when they surface. But when we actively consult the source, we can take the next step of correctly processing those memories.

If our memories promote self-doubt and attempt to steal our focus on serving God, consider the source. If our memories are focused on killing one's joy, consider the source. If the recall of our memories attempts to destroy our faith in the Father who loves us most, consider the source. These memories are not from God. Once identified, we can easily hand those over to God. We can take them to our Father in prayer and ask for His reassurance that He is not the source. We can then rely on Jesus and the Holy Spirit to combat these attacks for us, so we can ultimately find rest in their loving protection.

However, if memories of your past experiences make you thank God for where you are today, consider the source. If your memories bring you wisdom and guidance to avoid similar pitfalls from the past, consider the source. If your memories help strengthen your identity in Christ so that your forward mission in service to Him is unimpeded, consider the source. Here, there is no doubt that these memories are from God, used by the Holy Spirit to produce one or more of the fruits to further our relationship with Him. That in and of itself is a reason to worship the Lord even more.

Identifying the source promotes focus. And focused worship allows us to come into His presence with thanksgiving and a joyful heart. That is the moment when His peace and love simply invade and consume your space. For, at that moment, you will be in true worship, and His mercies and steadfast love will continue to be new every morning.

CHAPTER FOCUS:

1. Worship, worship, worship.
2. Let the Holy Spirit "bring to your remembrance all the things that I have said to you" to keep you focused during your daily worship.
3. Embrace your memories so you can genuinely see the source.
4. Take your memories to God.
   a. Praise Him for the memories He provides.

 b. Let Him have the memories that are not from Him, so Jesus and the Holy Spirit can go to battle with the enemy on your behalf.

5. Supporters, do not judge friends for their memories; instead, share in them for God's glory and purpose.

LIVING OUT THE LEGACY

Moving forward is probably the hardest component of passing through times of grief, sorrow, and loss. We often quip that time is the one thing that provides healing to all things. But if time truly healed all wounds, reliance on God would not be necessary. Counseling or other types of support would have no purpose. All we would need to do is lie in bed, pull the covers over our heads, and await the alarm clock of time to wake us when we have achieved complete healing.

Most friends and loved ones want to help relieve the pain suffered when we face times of grief and sorrow. The world wants nothing more than for us to arrive at that pivotal point where we are "over it." But all of us know in our hearts there are storms in our lives we will never get over, pain we seem destined to relive. Hopefully, you can see what was stated early on in this book. Getting over it is not required. Getting through it is the only way God can strengthen us and provide the courage to keep moving forward.

Each one of us has a legacy. Our legacy is in a constant state of construction throughout each season of our lives. Our morals and ethics, dreams and desires, and love for one another are just a few things that make up our personal legacy. How we handle success and failure, manage joyful moments, and even navigate loss all play into the construction of that very legacy.

Like myself, most want nothing more than for our legacy to live on long past our time on this earth—a great notion while we are living, no doubt. But living in the legacy of those closest to us who have realized their life's end is one of the most significant challenges we can face. But we can live on. And in doing so, we can find peace and joy living in the legacy of love left behind by those who have passed before us.

Romans 8:28 shows that God desires to use our times of grief and sorrow for our ultimate good—to land us in a place of peace, where we can choose to live in our loved one's legacy.

> 28 And we know that all things work together for good to those who love God, to those who are the called according to His purpose.

I realize that this can be one of the toughest verses to swallow when faced with a heartbreaking loss. Quoting this verse to a parent making funeral arrangements for their child is usually met with a much different viewpoint. Fortunately, this scripture declares a process that eventually allows us peaceful joy, knowing that God is still in control. The most important takeaway is understanding that this verse does not say God causes all things. What it says, and what we must grasp, is regardless of the cause or size of the heartache, God has the power to turn all things into good for those who love God. God is the only one powerful enough to use love over time to change the circumstance from tragedy to triumph. The good that comes out is your legacy. The process we go through to get there must include continual worship.

To further this point, James also reminds us that times of tribulation have a purpose. James 1:2–4 boldly states:

> [2]My brethren, count it all joy when you fall into various trials, [3]knowing that the testing of your faith produces patience. [4]But let patience have its perfect work, that you may be perfect and complete, lacking nothing.

Once again, we are provided with a process that produces our needed outcome. Trials in our lives set off a chain reaction—one that may start with sorrow and grief but end in a lack for nothing. I admit, another verse challenging to grasp when in the throes of immense grief and sorrow. But if we see the process, we can understand the one crucial point made earlier. Nowhere in this verse does James state God is the cause of our various trials or the tester of our faith. But when our faith is tested, patience is produced. And as time passes, it is patience that manufactures the outcome. It is patient reliance and trust that your heavenly Father is walking with you, not against you. And with that, patience's perfect work will make you whole again. And once there, we find that, though we may have lost something or someone in our lives, we still lack nothing. Yes, managing our trials and the associated grief and sorrow requires a process, and that process does take time. But if we can keep our faith focused on our Father's love, the tragedy can only end in victory.

Throughout this journey, we have discussed how sorrow is a part of our earthly lives. It exists and serves a purpose. We saw Jesus Himself profess to His disciples that they would experience immense sorrow because of His crucifixion. But He promised, upon seeing Him again, a joy no one can steal. Jesus, in John 10:10, further substantiated His overall mission:

> [10]... I have come that they may have life, and that they may have it more abundantly.

What is Jesus doing in these two circumstances that declare life in abundance and a provision of joy no one can steal? He is establishing

His legacy for us—the legacy He wants us to enjoy now on earth and one that we will continue to experience throughout eternity with Him. What is more significant is that Jesus's legacy was meant to be passed on to others through us—a legacy grounded in love, meant to be shared with those around us, as seen clearly in John 15:11–12.

> [11]These things I have spoken to you, that My joy may remain in you, and that your joy may be full. [12]This is my commandment, that you love one another as I have loved you.

And Jesus promises to validate the times we choose to live out His legacy. Mathew 25:34–40 provides us with that validation to come.

> [34]Then the King will say to those on His right hand, "Come, you blessed of My Father, inherit the kingdom prepared for you from the foundation of the world: [35]for I was hungry and you gave Me food; I was thirsty and you gave Me drink; I was a stranger and you took Me in; [36]I was naked and you clothed Me; I was sick and you visited Me; I was in prison and you came to Me.' [37]" Then the righteous will answer Him, saying, "Lord, when did we see You hungry and feed You, or thirsty and give You drink? [38]When did we see You a stranger and take You in, or naked and clothe You? [39]Or when did we see You sick, or in prison, and come to You?" [40]And the King will answer and say to them, "Assuredly, I say to you, inasmuch as you did it to one of the least of these My brethren, you did it to Me."

Just as Jesus left a tremendous legacy of love for us, realized by an abundant life with full and remaining joy, I believe our past loved ones have left a similar legacy. I further believe that our sorrow and grief are a barometer of the amount of love we had for them. Our sadness over their passing would not exist at all if we did not have a love for them. When we can see our sorrow as a measuring stick of love, I believe we are continuing to honor and love them in the same manner Jesus loves us.

We all have a legacy we are working on. It is called our life. And most of us would love nothing more than to have our life's legacy live on long after we are gone. Though I have no ambitions a library will ever be named after me or a foundation will be started in my name for the greater good, people do similar things every day that further the legacy of those we have lost. I submit that anytime you effectively manage your memories as a means to find peaceful joy, you are living in your loved one's legacy. Anytime we live out the lessons, morals, or ethics instilled within us by a key figure in our life, we are living out their legacy. And anytime we transmit that love for someone else's benefit, not only are we living out their legacy, but we are also living out Jesus's legacy.

Living out the legacy starts with, continues with, and never ends in worship to our heavenly Father. Daily, steadfast, and continual worship is the key to finding peace, joy, and that abundant life that Jesus left for us in His legacy. Worshiping through the tears is challenging. It can be hard to imagine and at times difficult to grasp. But when we choose to worship even when tears fall, the legacy of love Jesus left us becomes the driving force behind the comfort the Holy Spirit provides. With that comfort comes peace, and peace results in joy. And before you know it, the legacy lives on more robustly than ever.

LIFE FOCUS:

1. Worship, worship, worship.
2. Embrace the memories that God provides.

3. Have the courage to live out the legacy of love God has left for you through Jesus and others closest to you.

4. Never stop the pursuit of passing on the legacy of love God is working in your life for the benefit of others.

RECOMMENDED SONGS FOR WORSHIP

Week 1:

Bethel Music. 2011. "God I Look to You." *Be Lifted High.*

Hillsong Worship. 1996. "I Give You My Heart." *God Is in the House.*

Hillsong Worship. 2009. "I Will Exalt You." *Faith + Hope + Love.*

Tomlin, Chris. 2011. "Lord I Need You." *Passion: Here For You.*

Week 2:

Hillsong UNITED. 2016. "What a Beautiful Name." *Let There Be Light.*

Bethel Music. 2019. "Goodness of God." *Without Words: Genesis.*

Casting Crowns. 2014. "Just Be Held." *Thrive.*

Battistelli, Francesca. 2014. "Holy Spirit." *If We Were Honest.*

Week 3:

Tomlin, Chris. 2018. "Praise Is the Highway." *Holy Roar.*

Tomlin, Chris. 2016. "Good Father." *The Ultimate Playlist.*

Redman, Matt. 2015. "Unbroken Praise." *Unbroken Praise.*

Brymer, David, Onething. 2012. "Worthy of It All." *Magnificent Obsession.*

Week 4:

Bethel Music. 2019. "Raise a Hallelujah." *Without Words: Genesis.*

Battistelli, Francesca, All Sons and Daughters. 2014. "Tonight." *If We're Honest.*

Waller, John. 2007. "While I'm Waiting." *The Blessing.*

Grant, Amy. 1980. "All I Ever Have to Be." *Never Alone.*

Week 5:

Vertical Worship. 2018. "Yes I Will." *Bright Faith Bold Future.*

Rend Collective. 2015. "Joy of the Lord." *As Family We Go.*

All Sons and Daughters. 2013. "Great Are You Lord." *Live.*

Elevation Worship. 2019. "See a Victory." *At Midnight.*

Week 6:

DiMarco, Kristene. Bethel Music. 2017. "Take Courage." *Starlight.*

Cook, Amanda. Bethel Music. 2014. "You Make Me Brave." *Live at the Civic.*

West, Matthew. 2017. "All In." *All In.*

Hester, Benny. 1988. "Legacy." *Personal Best.*

WORKS CITED

1. *Occupational Outlook Handbook>Community and Social Service,* September 1, 2020, https://www.bls.gov/ooh/community-and-social-service/substance-abuse-behavioral-disorder-and-and-mental-health-counselors.htm.
2. *Behavioral Therapist in the US Market Size 2002–2025,* accessed October 15, 2020, https://www.ibisworld.com/industry-statistics/market-size/behavioral-therapists-united-states/.
3. Oleg Shukalovich, *Bible and Strong's Concordance,* Application, accessed November 1, 2020.